A Robbie Reader

MONEY MATTERS: A KID'S GUIDE TO MONEY

# BUDGETING TIPS FOR KIDS

Tamra Orr

Mitchell Lane
PUBLISHERS

P.O. Box 196
Hockessin, Delaware 19707
Visit us on the web: www.mitchelllane.com
Comments? email us: mitchelllane@mitchelllane.com

*Mitchell Lane*
**PUBLISHERS**

# MONEY MATTERS
# A KID'S GUIDE TO MONEY

**Budgeting Tips for Kids**

**A Kid's Guide to Coin Collecting**

**A Kid's Guide to Earning Money**

**A Kid's Guide to Stock Market Investing**

**Savings Tips for Kids**

**ABOUT THE AUTHOR:** Tamra Orr is the author of more than 100 books for children of all ages. She lives in the Pacific Northwest with her four kids and husband and has become an expert at family budgeting. She did not learn how to budget until she was married and wishes someone had shown her a book like this when she was much younger. Being an author is the best possible job she can imagine.

**PUBLISHER'S NOTE:** The facts on which the story in this book is based have been thoroughly researched. Documentation of such research can be found on page 46. While every possible effort has been made to ensure accuracy, the publisher will not assume liability for damages caused by inaccuracies in the data, and makes no warranty on the accuracy of the information contained herein.

Library of Congress Cataloging-in-Publication Data

Orr, Tamra.
  Budgeting tips for kids / by Tamra Orr.
    p. cm. —(Money matters—a kid's guide to money)
  Includes bibliographical references and index.
  ISBN 978-1-58415-644-4 (library bound)
  1.  Children—Finance, Personal—Juvenile literature.  I. Title.
  HG179.O763 2009
  332.0240083—dc22
                                        2008002268

**Printing**   1   2   3   4   5   6   7   8   9

PLB

# Contents

# THE NEW ART TEACHER

"Hey, Hannah! Good morning," Michael shouted as he yanked open his locker.

"Hey, Michael," she replied. "How was your weekend?"

"It was okay. I wanted to buy a new game for my Playstation® system, but I ran out of money," said Michael. "You know how that goes."

Hannah grinned. "Oh, yeah. The bucks always run out too fast, don't they?"

When the bell rang, Hannah slammed her locker shut. She wasn't worried about being late—her locker was right next to her classroom. She dashed through the door and headed for her desk. As she sat down, she glanced to the front of the room and smiled at Mrs. Hathaway. Her teacher didn't seem to see her. In fact, Mrs. Hathaway looked rather troubled. Hannah's smile faded. What could be wrong?

After everyone had settled in and taken their seats, Mrs. Hathaway stood in front of the class with a solemn face. "I know that many of you have been following the story about our school getting a new part-time art teacher," she said. Several students nodded. Everyone loved art class, and this new teacher was rumored to be able to teach them all kinds of new things, like soap carving, sculpting with clay, and painting huge murals with watercolors.

"I heard he's coming all the way from somewhere on the East Coast," said Kevin.

"I heard he's won a bunch of important awards for some of his sculptures," added Leila. "I also heard that some of his work is on display in big art galleries."

Mrs. Hathaway nodded. "You're right about all those things. However, there's a chance that Mr. Simmons may not be joining our school after all."

The classroom erupted in questions, complaints, and confusion. The teacher put her hand up, and immediately the students quieted down again.

"I know this is a real disappointment to you. Believe me, it is a disappointment to all of us."

Julio raised his hand. "Did Mr. Simmons take a job with some other school?" he asked.

"Oh, no," explained Mrs. Hathaway. "The reason he may not be able to come here boils down to dollars and cents. The school is in the midst of trying to

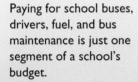

Paying for school buses, drivers, fuel, and bus maintenance is just one segment of a school's budget.

balance its yearly budget, and they are having some trouble. There may not be enough funds to bring in a new teacher, even part time. It will be a hard decision for the school board to make."

"What's a budget?" asked Christine. "And how do you balance it? Is it heavy?"

"Can we do anything about it?" asked Ronaldo.

"Those are both good questions," said Mrs. Hathaway. "I decided last night that we should talk about budgets this week in class. That will help you understand why the school makes some of the decisions it does. It might also show us some ways that we can make a difference, Ronaldo," She took a breath. "First, let's start with a homework assignment."

The students groaned. Mrs. Hathaway smiled back.

"It's not a difficult one," she assured them. "I simply want you to go home tonight and ask your mom or dad about the family budget. Ask them to sit down and explain how they make one, if they do. Learn as much as you can about how

Sitting down and talking to each other about how best to spend money and follow a budget is one of the things many families do. When you can stick to a budget, you can keep yourself out of financial trouble.

Have you ever seen one of your parents sit down and write a check? They are most likely paying a monthly bill. Some bills are paid online, some in person, some by check sent through the mail.

they do it, and then write it down. You don't have to ask exactly how much money they make, just how they figure it out. In the coming days, we will talk about different styles as we learn more about what a budget is. We will also create our own classroom budget."

Mrs. Hathaway walked up to the blackboard. "For the rest of this hour, let's make a list—the first step in understanding budgets. Now, what expenses do you think our school has to pay each month?"

Many hands went up.

"The electricity we need for our lights and computers," volunteered Cameron.

"The books we use in the classroom and in the library," stated Leslie.

"The food in the cafeteria, horrible as it may be," said Carmen, laughing. Everyone giggled.

Mrs. Hathaway wrote each one of these ideas down. By the end of class, there were a dozen words on the list.

| telephones | electricity |
| computers | books |
| principal | food |
| papers | heat |
| sports equipment | teachers |
| water | janitors |

Spending your money wisely is the first key to having enough to stick to a budget in the first place.

"What a great start!" exclaimed Mrs. Hathaway. "For the rest of the week, we will explore the different parts of a budget and why having one makes life easier for most people. Then we will talk about how to balance one. It can be heavy, Christine, but not in the way you think."

Just then the bell rang. "Remember to talk to your parents tonight," Mrs. Hathaway reminded her students as they filed to their next class. Hannah glanced back as she went out the door. It made her happy to see her favorite teacher smiling again.

# BUDGET BASICS

Have you ever heard your parents or other adults mention budgets? Perhaps you have heard the word mentioned on the news when there is a story about the government.

The word *budget* comes from the French word *bougette*, which means "leather purse." In English, it has come to mean "a list of planned **income** and **expenses**." A budget is a detailed plan of what money comes into your purse or wallet and then what goes out again.

In some ways, a budget is like a financial report card. It tells you how well you are doing financially. Instead of grades, though, it keeps track of what money you bring in (**income**), what money goes out (**expenses**), and how much you have left when you have met your expenses. Income sources are any places from which your money comes: allowance, payment for extra chores, gift money. For adults, expense categories might include rent or mortgage, food, electricity, phone, and entertainment. For kids, expenses might include after-school snacks, presents for friends, video games, and big-ticket items such as a Wii™ or Playstation® gaming system.

Why is a budget such a big deal? It will give you power over your money, instead of your money overpowering you. For example:

## Money Makers

Experts say that the number one reason a budget does not work is a bad attitude about it. If you think about keeping track of your money as depressing or too difficult, it isn't likely to work. Picture it as a money game instead—with you as the winner every time.

- You'll know exactly how much money you have to work with each month (income).
- You'll know exactly how much money you spend each month (and this can be a really eye-opening experience for anyone!).
- You'll be able to see which expenses can and cannot be changed so that you spend less.
- You'll know if you need to find new ways to make money.
- You'll be able to save money realistically for big-ticket items.

Learning how to handle your money may not seem all that important to you now. You're probably still in school and living at home, with plans for how to spend your next six months' worth of allowance. However, by learning about budgets, you will find more meaningful things to do with that allowance. You will also find budgeting important in the future, when you live on your own and have a lot more responsibility. Learning how to put together a **reliable** budget now will make it much easier to do so again in the future. You will have a great head start for when you are on your own and cannot depend on others to pay for things you need.

Many people have trouble sticking to a budget. They often rely on credit cards to help them pay their bills. But if they can't pay off their credit cards every month, they can find themselves in big trouble.

Planning a vacation can be a lot of fun for you and your family. Along with figuring out where you want to go, of course, your parents will also be figuring out how much the vacation will cost and how it will fit into the family budget.

One of the hardest lessons for some people (of all ages!) to learn is how to make sure they balance the money coming in with the money going out. This is known as balancing the budget. The struggle is understandable! It is usually much easier to spend money than it is to earn it—more fun, too.

However, the fun comes to an end quickly if you need money for something and you do not have it because you did not make a plan. A budget is a way to protect yourself from financial disappointment—and disaster.

How can a budget protect you from running out of money or help you save for some of the things you want the most? To find out, you have to learn all the details of your spending habits, including how much you earn and how much you spend and why. As you learn more about money, you will find out even more about yourself. Those are some of the most important lessons of all!

# WHAT COMES IN

# 3

Income is exactly that: the money coming in. For most adults, their income is what they receive as payment for doing their jobs. Most people get regular paychecks (once a week, twice a month, or some other schedule), and they use that dollar amount to set up their budgets. They may also be able to add money that they get from doing odd jobs or from various types of **investments**. Married couples may put their checks together and then use the total amount to pay their bills, or they may split the bills, with each person responsible for a different set.

PLAN AHEAD

What can you use to figure your income? Start with the money you get on a regular basis, such as allowance or money from a part-time job. You can also add in money that comes now and then, such as:

- birthday money
- holiday money
- money for occasional jobs
- coins you collect and turn into the bank

Take a look at your chart. Can you believe that it is possible to receive more than $100 a month?

| TYPES OF INCOME | AMOUNT | PER MONTH |
|---|---|---|
| Allowance | $10.00/wk | $40.00 |
| Part-time job | $15.00/wk | $60.00 |
| Extra gifts, etc. | $5.00/wk | $20.00 |

If your numbers are not this high, perhaps it is time to look at ways you can earn some additional money. What are some ways to do this? First, you could ask your parents if you may be paid to do extra chores around the house. Think about jobs that aren't already on your chore list. For example, you might take out the trash, babysit younger brothers and sisters, clean out the garage, or run errands.

Talk to your parents about what they need help with the most. Don't stop there, though. Ask others you know how you might help them. Talk to your neighbors. Call your grandparents or other relatives if they live nearby. Are there

One way to earn some extra money is to do extra chores around the house, such as folding laundry, mowing the yard, taking out the trash, or washing the dishes.

any elderly people in your area? Any families with a new baby? Often they need help doing things that would be easy for you to do. You would be helping someone and receiving some money for it—a win-win situation all around.

Other ways you can earn some extra money might be recycling plastic and glass items, tutoring other students, or selling things you no longer want (books you've read, clothes that are too small, or toys you've outgrown).

Along with making more money, it is important to spend less money. One way to try this is to begin paying less for what you buy. Start watching for coupons, sales, and **discounts** for the things you want to purchase. You can find special offers in stores, in your local newspaper, in magazines, and even online. Take advantage of them.

Also take time to **comparison shop**. This means looking at the same product at different places and see which one has the best price. If you see something you want for $25.00, for example, check out other stores to see what

USED CDs!

Buying something used can be a great way to save money. The most important key is to check out the product carefully. For example, if you are going to buy a used CD, take a look at it and make sure it does not have any scratches on it.

they are charging for the same product. Is anyone offering a discount? Go online and see if you can find it for less. Check out local ads to see if someone has what you want and is willing to sell it to you for a fraction of what you would pay for it new. Don't just jump at the deal, though: Make sure that used items are in good shape. Even if you pay a small price for it, if it

FINAL
clearance
50% off
all remaining clearance shoes

doesn't work, the money has been wasted. Comparison shopping may mean waiting a little longer to get what you want, but it almost always saves you money.

Now that you know what your income is, as well as ways to increase it if you want to, it's time to figure out your expenses, or **outgo**. This amount is often a surprise, too. Even when you just spend a few dollars here and there, the money can add up fast.

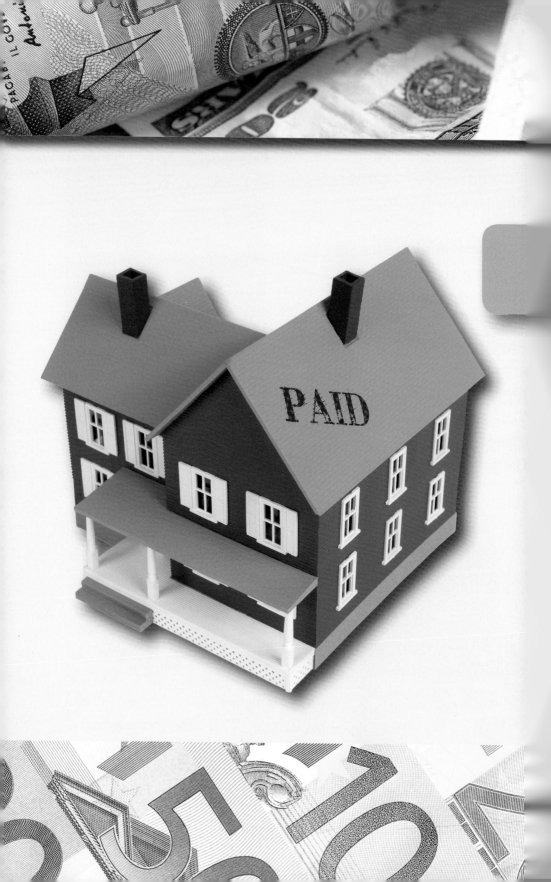

# WHAT GOES OUT

Now that you know how much money you have coming in each week or month, it is time to figure out how much you spend in the same time period. Most people think they spend very little money, but by keeping track of it for a few weeks, they find out otherwise.

Just as adults typically bring in more money than young people, they also have far more bills to pay with it. For example, their paychecks usually have to cover the following, every month:

- food—groceries and eating out
- rent/mortgage
- car payments
- gasoline
- car maintenance
- car insurance
- health insurance
- life insurance

Families have to budget for keeping the family car, truck, or van in good shape. Paying someone to fix them can be expensive, so many parents learn how to do basic maintenance on their own.

- house insurance
- telephones—house phones and cell phones
- electricity
- heat
- water
- sewage
- trash

- clothes/shoes/haircuts
- computer service
- cable/satellite dish
- taxes (property, license plate, etc.)
- home repairs and improvements
- entertainment—renting movies, bowling, golfing, etc.

Did you have any idea that a family could have that many bills to pay every month? No wonder most adults have to work full-time. Some families may even have additional bills, such as bank loans, credit card debt, or child care. It is often hard, even for adults, to stick to a budget and stay within their income limits. When a person spends more than they earn, they become **overextended**—and it is very hard to dig out of that hole.

Where does *your* money go? One of the best ways to find out is to write down every penny you spend for a month. If you are like most people, you do not really know where all your money goes. It just seems to disappear quickly, running out far faster than you had expected.

To make a budget, keep track of your expenses for one month. Here is an example of where you might be spending a few dollars here or there:

- snacks or drinks on the way home from school
- books, comic books, magazines, other reading material
- toys, games
- clothes
- gum, candy
- downloading songs for your MP3 player
- compact discs
- transportation (bus tickets, for example)
- movies

Downloading your music onto a handheld computer can add up to big bucks.

What else can you think of? Do you stop off anywhere on the way home from school? Play video games at an arcade? What do you do when you spend time with your friends? What hobbies and collections do you have? What do you do in your free time and on the weekends?

# Money Makers

For people who are addicted to shopping, it can be nearly impossible to stick to a budget. The problem is usually not a lack of money, but a lack of spending control.

Be sure to budget for a fun night out once in a while, such as roller skating with friends. If you find you're spending all your money on roller skating, though, you might need to consider skating less often.

Be sure to include any money you spend on any of these activities, too.

How can you keep such close track of what you spend? Start by getting a small spiral-bound notebook and a pen. The pen and notebook should be small enough to carry easily in your backpack, purse, or bag. Keep them with you wherever you go, because you will need to write in the notebook often. Don't make the mistake of thinking you can wait until the end of the day to write it down—it's too easy to forget.

Open your notebook and at the top of the page, write the day's date. Then divide the page into three columns. Label the columns Place, Item, and Amount. At the bottom, leave room for totaling the third column at the end of the day.

DATE: September 5

| PLACE | ITEM | AMOUNT |
|-------|------|--------|
| cafeteria | extra dessert with lunch | .75 |
| bookstore | bookmark and comic book | $5.33 |
| coffee shop | candy and soda | $1.19 |
| game store | connector cord | $10.46 |
| Tony | loan for his lunch | $2.25 |
| | TOTAL SPENT: | $19.98 |

Each day of the month should have its own page, so you should do this for 30 or 31 pages—depending on how long the month is. On the bottom of each page, total up the day's amounts.

Continue to do this each day for one month. Remember that some days you'll spend a lot more than others—for example, when you go roller skating or to the video arcade.

When you get to the end of the month, total the figures on each page. How much did you spend this month? How does it compare with your income? Now total up each

It's hard to believe that a little candy during the week can stress your budget, but keep track of how much you spend on it during an entire month and you may be in for a surprise.

type of spending you did. For example, during this month you spent $23.80 on food and drinks, $24.00 on books and magazines, and $40.00 on roller skating. This gives you a much clearer picture of exactly where your money is going. When you're finished, make another chart, like this one:

| ITEMS BOUGHT | SPENT PER MONTH |
|---|---|
| Drinks and food | $23.80 |
| Books and magazines | $24.00 |
| Roller rink | $40.00 |
| Games and toys | $31.00 |
| Loans to friends | $4.50 |
| Stuff from the school store | $4.00 |
| TOTAL SPENT FOR THE MONTH | $127.30 |

Are you amazed that you spent that much money in a month? In this second example, it comes to $127.30! Where did you spend the most money? Look at each of the columns carefully. Then ask yourself these questions:

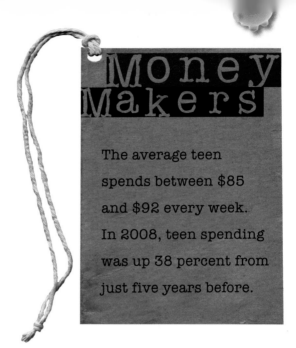

(1) What do I spend money on?
(2) Of those things, how many do I have to have?
(3) Which of these things can I easily give up?
(4) Of the ones I can give up, am I willing to stop buying them for a while to see what happens?

Think carefully about your answers. Can you try changing your habits today?

Keeping a careful record like this, as well as analyzing how you use your money, teaches you a great deal about your spending habits. The next step? Put it all together and see what you have left—or what you do not.

# PUTTING IT ALL TOGETHER

Now that you have a realistic picture of your income and expenses, you can see how well they balance. If you spend more than you take in, you will soon run out of money. While you might be able to live without a new game or snacks after school, it won't be much fun being broke if you have to stay home while your friends are out at the movies.

If your imbalance is the other way around, of course, you will have money left over. That can be a good thing and in fact, it can be a way to start saving for something big that you would like to buy.

Let's take a look at your income and expenses. In the examples in chapters 3 and 4, the monthly income was $120, and expenses were $127.30. If you subtract expenses from income, you get

$$\$120.00 \text{ (income)} - \$127.30 \text{ (expenses)} = -\$7.30$$

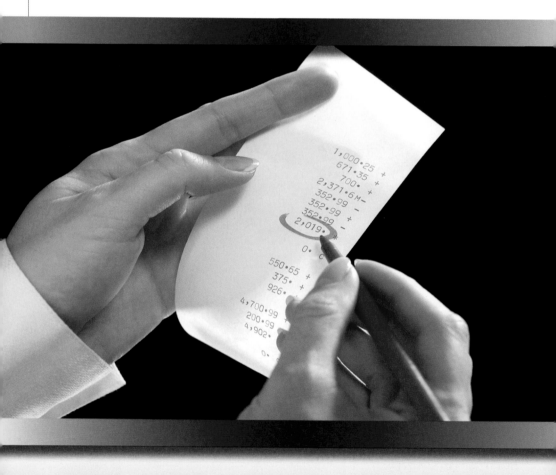

You might want to have a small calculator or adding machine in your room to help you keep close track of your income and outgo. Check the tape to make sure you put all the numbers in correctly.

If you budget carefully, you might be able to buy a video game and have fun battling your brother, sister, or friends.

You won't last a month with these spending habits. You would also never be able to save for a big-ticket item, like a Playstation® system, if you were constantly spending more than you earned.

When you set up a budget, you can see how to make changes that will allow you to reach that balance. And if you plan for a big-ticket item in your budget, you'll be able to save that much faster.

If you find you are "in the red"—meaning you have a negative balance at the end of the month—look for changes you can make that will put you "in the black"—back on the positive side.

Chapter 3 gives ideas for ways you

## Money Makers

Many **financial planners** will advise you to put away a certain amount of money as soon as you receive your pay. That way, it will be saved before you have the chance to spend it.

could increase your income, but sometimes finding extra income, or the time to earn it, can be tough to do. Another way to adjust your budget is to look at how you can decrease your expenses. For example, if you skip about half the snacks and drinks you usually buy on your way home from school, you would cut the cost from $23.80 to $11.90. If you redo the formula, you will see that now you have money left over.

$$\$120.00 \text{ (income)} - \$115.40 \text{ (expenses)} = + \$4.60$$

Just one change and you are already out of the red! If you cut down on how much you spend on games or on books and magazines, you would have even more.

If you saved $4.60 each month for a whole year, how much will you have saved?

$$\$4.60 \times 12 \text{ months} = \$55.20$$

$55.20! That is a lot of money. Think about what you could do with it, from putting it in the bank for college or giving it to a favorite **charity** or buying a new video game.

How can you help make sure you have enough income to meet your expenses? You might try setting up a system in your room. First, get out four envelopes (you can also use glass jars or plastic containers). Mark each one with where that money is supposed to go. You might mark them with:

A Money Savvy piggy bank is divided into four categories for you.

- everyday expenses
- savings
- new _____ (you fill in the blank with whatever you want to save for)
- gifts and charities

Typically, money experts suggest that you put 40 percent of your income into everyday expenses, 30 percent in savings, 20 percent for buying something big, and 10 percent in charities or gifts.

If you follow this formula, using the figures from the charts above, how much would you put in each container each month?

**Everyday Expenses**
$120.00 x 40 percent
= $48.00

**Savings For Small Items You'd Like to Have**
$120.00 x 30 percent
= $36.00

**Big Items (like a bicycle or MP3 player)**
$120.00 x 20 percent
= $24.00

**Gifts or Charities**
$120.00 x 10 percent
= $12.00

Once you start the habit of putting your money into these categories, you can begin to live with them on a daily basis. For example, if you know you have $48.00 a month for everyday expenses, and you divide by 30 days in a month, you'll see you have about $1.60 a day to spend. Of course, some days you will spend more and some days less, but together, those days should average $1.60 or less to keep to your budget.

Taking control of your money—what comes in and what goes out—is an important part of growing up. By starting to learn these lessons now, you will be well prepared for the day you are grown up and living on your own. When faced with bills to pay, you will know to grab those envelopes and start dividing up your paycheck. Balancing a budget will be a familiar trick that you will be able to do with ease!

## Money Makers

The 2005 Federal Budget Deficit of $521 billion would create a stack of $1 bills 35,931 miles high.

# What Did You Learn About Budgeting?

# MRS. HATHAWAY'S BUDGET

"What did you find out about budgets when you talked to your parents?" Mrs. Hathaway asked at the beginning of class the next day.

"I found out that there are a lot more things you have to pay for than I ever expected," said Kevin. "No wonder they always ask me to turn off the lights when I leave a room. Electricity is expensive."

"My mom showed me how she uses the envelope system to keep her money separated," added Christine. "I never knew she did that before."

Grocery List
- corn
- cucumber
- tomatoes
- lettuce
- skim milk
- fresh salmon
- flowers
- avacado
- mushrooms
- dried fruit
- crackers

"I spent an hour clipping coupons with my dad," said Julio. "You can save a lot of money on food if you do that before you go to the grocery store."

"My uncle and I sat down and wrote out a list of the things we spend money on each month that we don't really need," Leila explained. "Of course, our ideas of what we needed were not always the same."

Mrs. Hathaway smiled. "That's not unusual," she said. "Now, I did my homework too. I talked to the principal and asked him for a list of expenses our school has that we might also be able to do without. He gave me lots of information, and I'm hoping that if we put our heads together, we might find a way to get Mr. Simmons to come and teach here. Shall we give it a try?"

One way that many families save a few dollars here and there is by cutting coupons out of the local newspaper. When they take coupons to the grocery store, the cashier rings them up and the amount due goes down, down, down. When you're on a tight budget, coupons can be a lifesaver.

Everyone nodded. Eager faces looked at Mrs. Hathaway as she prepared to put numbers on the blackboard. She had to chuckle, too. She had never seen her students so enthusiastic about doing math!

"Hey," Michael whispered to Hannah. "Do you think our new lesson will show me how to get that Playstation® game?"

"It could!" replied Hannah. "It just might be the solution we all need!"

## Books

Brookson, Stephen. *Essential Managers: Managing Budgets.* London: DK Publishing, 2000.

Gardner, David, et al, *The Motley Fool Investment Guide for Teens: 8 Steps to Having More Money Than Your Parents Ever Dreamed Of.* Alexandria, Virginia: Fireside, 2002.

Patton, Eliabeth A. *The Big Bucks: How to Manage Money Now That You're on Your Own.* Nashville, Tennessee: Thomas Nelson, 2002.

Shelley, Susan. *The Complete Idiot's Guide to Money for Teens.* New York: Alpha, 2001.

## Works Consulted

Bochner, Arthur, and Rose Bochner. *The New Totally Awesome Money Book for Kids.* New York: New Market Press, 2007.

"Explaining the Budget to Your Kids." Kiplinger, March 20, 2003
http://www.kiplinger.com/basics/managing/kids/budget.htm

Sander, Peter J. *The Pocket Idiot's Guide to Living on a Budget.* New York: Alpha, 2005.

"In the Money: U.S. Currency Trivia." Save Wealth.com
http://www.savewealth.com/specialreports/moneytrivia/

Shim, Jae. *Budgeting Basics and Beyond.* Hoboken, New Jersey: Wiley, 2005.

Walker, Tim. *America's Growing Debt: Understanding the Budget Deficit.* Alexandria, Virginia: Close Up Foundation, 1994.

## On the Internet

How To Teach Budgeting To Kids
http://www.howtodothings.com/finance-and-money/a2653-how-to-teach-budgeting-to-kids.html

PBS Kids: It's My Life: School, Time Management, Making a Budget
http://pbskids.org/itsmylife/school/time/article3.html

PBS Kids: It's My Life: Money
http://pbskids.org/itsmylife/money/index.html

Kiplinger: Household Budget Worksheet
http://www.kiplinger.com/tools/budget/

**charity** (CHAH-rih-tee)—An organization that helps people in some way; for example, by providing food for the homeless.

**comparison shop** (kum-PAYR-ih-sun SHOP)—Looking at the price of an item at different sources to know who is selling the item at the lowest price.

**discount** (DIS-kownt)—A reduced price.

**expenses** (ek-SPEN-ses)—The money that one spends; outgo.

**financial planner** (fy-NAN-chul PLAN-er)—A person who helps people figure out how to meet expenses and save for the future.

**income** (IN-kum)—The money received for goods or services (employment).

**inflation** (in-FLAY-shun)—The gradual increase in prices over time.

**investments** (in-VEST-ments)—Property or shares in a company that are bought with an eye for reselling later at a profit.

**outgo** (OUT-goh)—Money paid out, or amount spent.

**overextended** (oh-vur-ek-STEN-ded)—Having more money due to go out than is coming in.

**reliable** (ree-LY-uh-bul)—Dependable; able to be counted on.